Teaching English as a Foreign Language

A Guidebook for Primary Teachers

Nicole Rasool

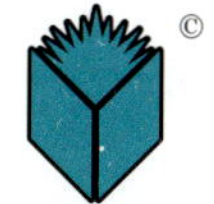

Paramount Publishing Enterprise

Karachi | Lahore | Islamabad | Faisalabad | Peshawar | Abbottabad | Hyderabad

Teaching English as a Foreign Language

by

Nicole Rasool

Published by

Paramount Publishing Enterprise

152/O, Block-2, P.E.C.H.S., Karachi-75400, Pakistan

Tel: 34310030, Fax: 34553772, E-mail: paramount@cyber.net.pk

Web site: www.paramountbooks.com.pk

ISBN: 978-969-494-945-1

Retail Price Rs.: 495.00

Printed in Pakistan

TABLE OF CONTENTS

Preface

Teaching English as a Foreign Language (EFL) can be a highly complex process that leaves teachers confused and unsure, especially if the teacher has had very little exposure to English herself. With this in mind, I set out to develop a guidebook that can help guide teachers every step of the way as they craft their own EFL programs for elementary students. In the development of this guidebook, extensive research has been done, in order to produce the most effective teaching practices for EFL students. Also, recommendations are made based on my own teaching experience as an EFL teacher in Pakistani elementary classrooms, as well as previous teaching experience in American classrooms. In this text, I hope to create a feeling that demonstrates an utmost respect for teachers as knowledgeable professionals, who are lifelong learners, always in search of improvement in their own teaching skills as well as improvement in the skills of their students.

How the Book is Organized

The book begins with the introduction of some basic concepts of EFL teaching that every elementary teacher should know. Then, an overall view of how to design an EFL program is discussed. Next, reading, vocabulary, writing, and oral language are discussed independently. Finally, the book concludes with a suggested weekly EFL plan for a 1st grade classroom with daily lesson plans. Included in the appendices is a list of EFL materials that are available in Pakistan, as well as a list of useful EFL websites for teachers and students.

LIST OF TABLES

LIST OF FIGURES

Basic Concepts of EFL Teaching

In order to develop an effective EFL program, teachers need to be knowledgeable of some basic EFL concepts which include: (a) comprehensible input, and (b) developmental stages of English language learning. Teachers also must develop a curriculum that focuses on ALL strands of English which include: (a) reading, (b) writing, (c) vocabulary, (d) grammar, (e) spelling, and (f) oral language. With this knowledge, teachers can prepare more effective lesson plans that meet the needs of their EFL students.

Comprehensible Input

Comprehensible Input is a concept developed by Krashen in 1981 (as cited in Gipe, 2006) and includes teaching practices that specifically help English Language Learners (ELLs) acquire English more easily. Listed in Table 1 are the types of teaching practices that teachers should employ when they help EFL students in the classroom.

Table 1

Ensuring Comprehensible Input

1. Use visuals.
2. Use gestures and body language.
3. Speak slowly and enunciate.
4. Use longer and natural pauses at phrase and sentence boundaries.
5. Use natural redundancy in speaking by providing more than one explanation of an idea; repeat and review often.
6. Exaggerate intonation at appropriate times.
7. Use simpler syntax.
8. Stress high frequency vocabulary.
9. Maintain a low anxiety level.
10. Stress participatory learning.
11. Clarify meaning through context, definition, or paraphrasing.
12. Use fewer idioms and slang, and avoid culturally-bound clichés and metaphors.
13. Be enthusiastic and use a warm voice.
14. Use shorter sentences.

Information source: Gipe, J. (2006). Multiple Paths to Literacy. Assessment and differentiated instruction for diverse learners, K-12. (6th ed.). Upper Saddle River, NJ: Pearson Education (p.49).

Developmental Stages of English Language Development

When students acquire a second language, they experience five different developmental stages (Gipe, 2006). Listed in Table 2 are: (a) the five different levels, (b) characteristics of learners at each different level, and (c) the recommended instructional strategies. Please note that some strategies may be effective in several different levels and teachers need to gauge the needs of their learners to understand which strategies are best; however, the following can be used as a general guide.

Table 2

Developmental Stages of English Language Development

Stage	Characteristics		Instructional Strategies
1 Beginner	Becomes familiar with English sounds, rhythm, and patterns	o	Use visuals, props, and real objects
		o	Shared readings with visual support (felt board, puppets)
	Relies on picture clues for understanding during shared readings	o	Use language through songs, chants, and simple poems
		o	Cooperative learning groups
		o	Active listening
	Shows some comprehension of the gist of the language	o	Use physical movement in language activities (e.g., Total Physical Response [Asher, 1982])
		o	Use art, music, dance and pantomime to represent meaning
	Responds with one-word answers and by pointing, gesturing, nodding, drawing	o	Use the Language Experience Approach for Literacy
2 Early Intermediate	Confidence increases; speaks with less hesitation	o	Provide opportunities for oral language
	Listens with greater understanding	o	Use yes/no and either/or questions
	Identifies people, places, and objects	o	Ask problem-solving questions (who, what, where, when, why)
	Uses routine expressions	o	Label pictures and objects
	Can repeat and recite memorable language	o	Use shared readings with a variety of text genres
		o o	Use guided reading Ask open-ended questions

3 Intermediate	Produces grammatically accurate phrases/sentences	o Oral presentations for an audience (author's chair, Readers Theater, content area projects)
	Experiments with new vocabulary in spoken English	o Present a variety of resource materials (textbooks, trade books, newspapers, dictionaries, etc.)
		o Conduct conferences with students to discuss progress in reading and writing
		o Use visuals and graphic organizers to make content information more accessible
		o Facilitate group discussions
4 Early Advanced	Produces connected discourse	o Use literature circles
	Uses more extensive vocabulary	o Introduce use of reference material for research
	Uses language to persuade and evaluate	o Request creative oral and written narratives
	Understands both narrative and expository material with greater depth	o Use writer's workshop to produce student-authored newsletters, bulletins, stories, poems and reports o Provide opportunities for performance-based assessment through art, music, dance, and drama
	Engages in research projects	o Integrated thematic units for content area subjects o Real-world literacy experiences to include classroom newsletters, pen pals, letters to the editor, creative writing contests and so on
5 Advanced	Understands idiomatic expressions Includes more creative and analytical writing using standard forms Language comparable to native English speakers of the same age	

Information source: Gipe, J. (2006). *Multiple paths to literacy. Assessment and differentiated instruction for diverse learners, K-12. (6th ed.)*. Upper Saddle River, NJ: Pearson Education (p 59-60).

How to Organize Your EFL Program?

When teachers develop an EFL Program, they must address all strands of English in order to create a successful EFL program. A well-developed program includes instruction in: (a) reading, (b) writing, (c) vocabulary, (d) grammar, (e) spelling, and (f) oral language.

Time

Optimally, students should receive 1 ½ hours of English instruction daily. 60 minutes should be devoted to reading, spelling, vocabulary, grammar, and oral language. 30 minutes should be reserved for writing. In particular, it is important to allow at least this amount of time for students in KG through 2nd grade.

Management of the 60-Minute Reading Time Block

Reading, spelling, vocabulary, grammar, and oral language should be taught within the first 60-minute time block of English instruction. Spelling, grammar, and vocabulary may be taught one to two times a week; however, reading and oral language need to be taught on a daily basis. In Table 3, you can see a simplified version of how to manage the time of this 60-minute block. More detailed information is included in Appendix A, Daily Lesson Plans for a 1st Grade Classroom.

Table 3
The 60-Minute Reading Time Block

Monday	Reading	Spelling	Vocabulary	Oral Language
Tuesday	Reading	Oral Language		
Wednesday	Reading	Vocabulary	Oral Language	
Thursday	Reading	Grammar	Oral Language	
Friday	Reading	Spelling	Oral Language	

What to Teach?

Teachers should choose materials that support a balanced approach to literacy instruction. In a balanced approach (Tompkins, 2001), students read authentic children's literature and also receive direct explicit instruction in phonemic awareness and phonics. Literacy-based instruction (Morrow, 2005) is the most recommended type of balanced reading program and includes direct instruction in: (a) reading, (b) vocabulary, (c) grammar, (d) spelling, and (e) oral language as they directly relate to an authentic piece of children's literature. Basal programs are another type of reading program in which students receive instruction in all strands of English; however, basal program literature is often of very low quality. If a basal program is required, it is recommended that teachers supplement the course with high quality children's literature, or choose a basal program that includes high quality literature.

What English Materials Should You Use?

What materials to use is quite a difficult task, especially in Pakistan. Unfortunately, there are not many good materials to choose from that are published in Pakistan, and imported products are just too costly for the average student to afford. Oxford University Press, from the United Kingdom, is the leading publisher of EFL materials in Pakistan. *Oxford Reading Tree* and *Oxford Literacy Web* are two reading programs with high quality children's literature that are available from Oxford; however, these programs are quite costly and often not available due to their high costs.

A very basic basal program called *New Oxford Modern English* by Nicholas Horsburgh (2009) is one program that addresses all strands of English teaching. Teachers can use this course as their main language program and then supplement it with readers and high quality children's literature. *New Oxford Modern English* is also published by Oxford University Press. If a school chooses this program as their main language program, it is of utmost concern that teachers supplement the program with additional literature. Also, Oxford publishes several different series of readers, fictional stories, and non-fictional literature that teachers can use to supplement their program. See Appendix B for a complete list of recommended teaching materials and children's literature.

Reading

What is the best way to teach reading? A combined approach that emphasizes the use of sight words and phonics is most recommended. Reading is an integral part of any EFL program and teachers should be knowledgeable of several concepts in reading in order to develop a successful program. Some of the most important concepts will be addressed here:

- Phonemic Awareness and Phonics
- High Frequency Words and Sight Words
- Types of Reading
- Comprehension

Phonemic Awareness and Phonics

Phonemic Awareness (Gipe, 2006) is the ability to understand that words are made up of sounds and those sounds can be manipulated. One type of phonemic awareness activity is when the teacher asks students to tell her words that begin with the

/c/ sound (the teacher says the sound only and not the letter). Students should begin phonemic instruction in the Pre-KG and KG classes and should receive a minimum of 18 hours of instruction before they advance to phonics instruction (National Reading Panel, 2000, as cited in Morrow, 2005). Phonemic awareness instruction should begin with rhymes and chants, and continue with blending and segmenting activities. Phonics is the study of words and letters and their associated sounds. Phonics instruction should begin after students have had adequate phonemic awareness instruction (Gipe, 2006). You can see the **Useful EFL Websites** section, page 85, for a website that offers readymade phonics worksheets. When teachers teach phonics, they should use the following guidelines:

- Teach phonics skills within children's literature in meaningful and purposeful ways. For example, if you are teaching the rime */in/*, choose a book that has a lot of words with 'in' at the end of the words. See Mitton in the reference list for a book with the rime */in/*.

- First, teach initial and final consonants. Initial consonants are all letters besides vowels that occur at the beginning of a word. Final consonants are all letters besides vowels that occur at the end of a word, i.e. **map, bat,** "m" and "b" are initial consonants, and "p" and "t" are final consonants.

- Then teach onsets and rimes, for example, */c/ and /at/* (cat) or */b/* and */at/* (bat), */h/* and */ot/* (hot), and */c/* and */ot/* (cot), etc. These are some common rimes: *at, ad, ag, ake, an, ash, ate, eat, ed, ell, en, est, et, ick, ight, ike, ill, im, in, ink, is, it, ock, og, oke, om, ot, uck, ug, up, us, ush, ut.* See below for a small mini lesson on how to teach onsets and rimes with the 'at' rime.

Teaching Onsets and Rimes

1. Teach students the sound that */at/* makes. Write it on the board and have them repeat the sound after you several times.

2. Now add a "c" in front of the "at" but slightly separated. Ask students what sound does "c" make as you point to it. They should respond */c/* .

3. Point to the "c" and then to the "at" as you encourage the students to say the sound of the onset and the rime with you. Have students repeat with you several times (pointing to the onset and the rime) as you narrow the gap between the two sounds until they are blended together and you hear the word, "cat".

4. Under the word "cat", write the rime */at/* again and add a "b" in front of the "at". Proceed with the same procedure as mentioned in steps 2 and 3.

5. Repeat steps 2 to 4 changing the onset to the following letters: *f, h, m.*

6. Now have students try and blend the onset and rime themselves and say the following words: pat, rat, sat. Write one word on the board at a time and ask a few students if they can read the word.

   ❖ Next, teach blends, two or more letters together that blend and make one sound ; however, the sounds of each of the letters can be heard, for example, */cl/, /tr/, /fl/, /str/*, etc. A great exercise is to have students circle the appropriate blend for the given picture. See Figure 1 for a worksheet on blends.

- Next, teach digraphs, two or more letters that combine together to make one sound and it is a completely different sound than the individual letters, e.g. */sh/, /ph/, /ch/, /gh/.* One great activity to use with digraphs is the use of riddles. Try this riddle activity below (Super Teacher Worksheets, 2009):

1. I start with sh.
   I have lots of wool.
   I am a farm animal.
   What am I?______________

2. I end with sh.
   You can count me.
   I am another word for money.
   What am I?______________

3. I end with ch.
   I rhyme with crunch.
   I am an afternoon meal.
   What am I?______________

4. I start with ch.
   I rhyme with lamp.
   I am a winner.
   What am I?______________

Answers: sheep, cash, lunch, champ,

- Next, teach vowels, first short vowels and then long vowels, e.g. a, e, i, o, u. Short vowel: */a/* as in cat. Long vowel: */i/* as in ice cream.

- Then, teach the three simple phonics rules. CV where the vowel is usually long (go, long, be, etc.),CVC (cat, bat, hot, etc.)and CVCe (plate,rule, etc.)

- Finally, teach vowel clusters (e.g. ai, ay, ea, ee, oi, oy, ew, ie, ei, etc.), prefixes (e.g. anti, auto, bi, in, non, pre, pro, sub, etc.), and suffixes (able, ate, ble, er, est, ful, ible, ment, some, tion, etc.)

Figure 1

Blends Worksheet

Circle the correct blend for the beginning sound of each picture and then write the blend on the line.

tr br

cl fl

High Frequency Words and Sight Words

High frequency words are words that appear most frequently in both children's and adult's literature (Gipe, 2006). Some high frequency words follow phonic patterns, however, others do not. Words that do not follow phonic patterns are termed Sight words. Students should learn high frequency words in a manner in which they will be able to automatically recognize words without having to try and decode them. It is advisable for children to learn the First 100 Most Frequently Used Words in the 1st grade. Table 4, contains the 100 most frequently used words according to Horn (1926, as cited in Tompkins, 2001).

Table 4

The 100 Most Frequently Used Words

a	about	after	all	am
an	and	are	around	as
at	back	be	because	but
by	came	can	could	day
did	didn't	do	don't	down
for	from	get	got	had
have	he	her	him	his
home	house	how	I	if
in	into	is	it	just
know	like	little	man	me
mother	my	no	not	now
of	on	one	our	or
out	over	people	put	said
saw	school	see	she	so
some	that	the	them	then
there	they	things	think	this
time	to	too	two	up
us	very	was	we	well
went	were	what	when	who
will	with	would	you	your

Information Source: Tompkins, G. (2001). *Literacy for the 21st century, a balanced approach.* **Upper Saddle River, N***J: Prentice-Hall, Inc. (p. 187)*

Teachers should keep in mind when they teach reading that although high frequency words and sight words are necessary in order to build students' fluency and automaticity, they are not the only means to teach reading. Teachers should also devote considerable time, especially in KG and 1st grade classes, to phonemic awareness and phonics instruction. Students begin reading by recognizing sight words automatically; however, they improve and grow their reading vocabulary through the use of decoding which utilizes phonic skills.

Types of Reading

Reading can be taught to the whole class, small groups of students, or individually. Typically, classrooms consist of 30+ children and individual instruction is not feasible. However, both whole class and small group, instruction is advised. Repeated reading, echo reading, reading aloud and independent reading are the most recommended methods of whole class instruction. Guided reading should be done in small groups. Teachers can organize their reading program by offering both whole class and small group instruction.

Given the fact that you have only 60 minutes daily devoted to reading and related activity work, teachers must decide which type of reading they will do each day. Guided reading is most effective as it allows the teacher to work with a small group of students (5-6 students), and thereby offer individualized instruction that will help each child improve his or her reading skills. However, whole class instruction can also be effective and some teachers may prefer whole class instruction as classroom management can be easier. Repeated reading, echo reading, and reading aloud can also be done in small groups as well as with the whole class. Each teacher will need to assess her class and her own teaching style to determine what type of reading will most benefit her class.

Repeated Reading (Gipe, 2006; Morrow, 2005; Tompkins, 2001) is a type of reading in which the students read the same text several times until they have become proficient in reading all the words correctly in the text. This type of reading can be done with the whole class or in small groups. This is a great type of reading for KG and 1st grade classes.

Echo Reading (Walker, 2003, as cited in Gipe, 2006) is a type of reading in which the teacher reads aloud one sentence at a time with the correct intonation and phrasing. The students then repeat the sentence in the same manner, while they read it from their own text. This process continues until the teacher feels confident that the students can repeat more than one sentence at a time. This type of reading can be done with the whole class or in small groups. Again, this type of reading is excellent for KG and 1st grade classes.

Independent Reading (Bamford & Day, 1997) is when students read text silently on their own. It is also referred to as "Silent Sustained Reading (SSR)" or "Drop Everything And Read" (DEAR). Students should participate in independent reading on a daily basis. Even young students in KG should have 5 to 10 minutes daily when they can explore books. During this time period, they can learn how to hold the book, turn the pages, and create stories for themselves based on the pictures. Older students should be given more time for independent reading than younger students (e.g. 1st grade students: 10 minutes; 5th grade students: 30 minutes). Teachers should hold students accountable (Morrow, 2005) for their reading and can do so when they have students: (a) create summaries based on their reading, (b) write about their favorite part of a book, or (c) have short individual conferences with the teacher.

Reading Aloud is when the teacher reads a text aloud to the students. This type of reading can be done with the whole class or small groups. Often, teachers will discuss the text before, during and after the reading to help reinforce students' comprehension skills. Reading aloud is a great way to increase students' vocabulary and it should be done on a daily basis in primary grades (i.e. KG - 3rd grade).

Guided Reading is a more complex reading process; however, it is the most effective method as well. In guided reading (Morrow, 2005), teachers break students up into 5-6 small groups. Each group consists of 5-6 students of similar literacy ability. The teacher works with one small group at a time, while the other groups participate in planned literacy centers set up around the classroom.

The teacher plans specific instruction to help improve the literacy skills of each of the small groups. Each group receives a different curriculum and reads different books. The teacher will choose books for each group that are too challenging for the students to read independently, but appropriate to use with the help of the teacher. She will then do guided reading, in which students in the small group that sit with the teacher, take turns as they read a small portion of the text at a time. The teacher guides each student as he or she reads and helps only when necessary.

The teacher uses several different reading strategies in the guided reading process such as the use of phonics skills, context skills, syntactic skills, or the use of pictures, to help children learn how to figure out the words on their own. A teacher must have very strong organizational and classroom management skills to be able to use this form of reading. However,this is the best type of reading instruction, as it directly improves students' reading skills based on individual assessment. You may refer to Appendix A and the lesson on small group reading instruction for more specific information on how to teach guided reading in small groups.

Comprehension

When students read material, the main goal is for the students to understand what they read (Gipe, 2006; Harvey & Goudvis, 2007; Tompkins, 2001). Comprehension is not a developmental skill that improves with time; rather, it is a teachable skill in which teachers must provide students with adequate strategies to become successful readers. There are several different types of reading strategies; however, the following are the most effective:

- Preview and Predict
- Accessing Prior Knowledge
- Monitoring Comprehension
- Summarizing
- Questioning
- Inferring
- Visualization

Teachers need to give students direct explicit instruction on how to use each of these strategies. Then, students should be allowed ample time for independent reading in order to practice using the given reading strategies. See Table 5 for a chart of reading strategies that teachers can enlarge and post in the classroom. Teachers should encourage students to refer to the chart often during reading.

When students preview and predict a text, they look at the title, pictures, headings, and subheadings and try to predict what the text will be about based on what they see. Students can predict what they think will happen next in the text throughout their reading, as well, and then confirm their predictions as they read the text.

Students use the strategy of accessing prior knowledge by relating things that have happened in their own life to things that happen in the text. If students have background knowledge about the subject in the text, they will better understand what they read.

Table 5

Reading Strategies Chart

	Reading Strategy	Example (Based on Big Bear's Bad Day by Celia Warren of Oxford Literacy Web)
	Preview and Predict- Look at the title, pictures, headings, and subheadings and try to predict what the text will be about based on what you see	Big Bear looks unhappy on the cover of the book. I think bad things will happen to him all day long.
	Accessing Prior Knowledge- What in my life is similar to that in the story? Have I read about something that is similar to this story?	I ride a bus to school also and one day I knocked over my friend's bottle.
	Monitoring Comprehension- Guessing, rereading, predicting, visualizing, questioning, personalizing	I don't know this word p-a-r-k, but I think it means park as it starts with p and the bear looks like he is at the park.
	Summarizing- Telling the main elements of the story	Bear goes on the bus and hits the cat by mistake. Then he goes to the park and hits another cat by mistake. Then he tries to go home, but misses his bus. Then cat gives him his glasses and he can now see.
?	Questioning- Asking questions to clarify the story	Why does bear keep hitting things? Is there something wrong with his eyes?
	Inferring- Drawing conclusions based on what you read	Bear won't hit anyone anymore because now he can see.
	Visualization- Making a picture in your head	Bear is at the park and there are swings, slides, trees, and animals there.

As students read, they should employ the reading strategy of monitoring their comprehension. See Table 6 for specific strategies students should use while they read.

Table 6

Comprehension Monitoring Strategies

1. Making a picture in one's mind about the text.
2. Asking one's self questions about the text.
3. Personalizing the text based on one's own experience.
4. Predicting from pictures, subtitles, and words during reading.
5. Going back and rereading when the text doesn't make sense.
6. Guessing the meaning of words during reading.

Information source: Gipe, J. (2006). *Multiple paths to literacy. Assessment and differentiated instruction for diverse learners,* K-12. (6th ed.). Upper Saddle River, NJ: Pearson Education (p.301).

Summarizing is when students list the important elements of a story or expository text. Teachers should instruct students that a good story includes the following elements: (a) main character and other characters, (b) setting, (c) problem, (d) plot or events of the story, and (e) conclusion/resolution. The strategy of summarizing can be done orally or written. See Table 7 for an example of a story map that was used as a comprehension assessment and was completed orally by a 9-year-old girl. A score of 80% or higher on the story map assessment is an acceptable comprehension level.

Table 7

Story Map for Assessment

Name: Aneesa Khan **Grade:** 4th **Date:** June 9th, 2011
Story Title and Author: Missing One Stuffed Rabbit by Maryann Cocca-Leffler.

Context: Story read by child __X__ Story read to child____ Child wrote the summary ______ Child orally told the summary __X__

Main Points for summarizing:

Characters: Janine, Mrs. Robin, kids in class, Janine's family, people in hospital
Child's response: The girls, the rabbit, the teacher, the students, and the dad and mom

Points: 6/6

Setting: School, Janine's home, the shopping mall, the hospital
Child's response: School, home, lunch, hospital________

Points: 12/12

Problem: Janine lost Coco
Child's response: The girl lost the rabbit ___

Points: 6/6

Plot/ Events: (Check those events the child retold. 6 points for each event.) 36 total

1. Mrs. Robin gave Coco to Janine for the weekend. **Yes**
2. Janine took Coco home and did everything with him. **Yes**
3. Janine went with her family to the mall and she lost Coco in the mall. **No, partial**
4. Janine had to go to school without Coco and tell everyone she had lost him. **Yes**
5. Janine and her classmates put up posters for lost Coco in the mall. **No, partial**
6. Janine and her classmates go to the hospital and find that Coco had been given to a sick little girl and they all decided Coco was where he should be. **No, partial**

Event points: 20/36

Conclusion/ Resolution: (6 points)
They find Coco at the hospital with a sick little girl and decide that Coco is where he should be. Yes points 6/6

Points: Total child received 50 / 66 = 76% /100

Adapted from: Gipe, J. (2006). *Multiple paths to literacy. Assessment and differentiated instruction for diverse learners, K-12. (6th ed.).* Upper Saddle River, NJ: Pearson Education. (p.112).

Also, see Table 8 for a story map form that students in 2nd grade and higher can use to begin to learn how to summarize a story.

Table 8

Story Map Form

Story Map

Name:__________ **Grade:**__________ **Date:**__________

Story Title and Author: ____________________

____

Characters: ____________________

Setting: ____________________

Problem: ____________________

Plot/ Events: ____________________

____

____

____

Conclusion/ Resolution:

Adapted from: Gipe, J. (2006). *Multiple paths to literacy. Assessment and differentiated instruction for diverse learners, K-12. (6th ed.).* Upper Saddle River, NJ: Pearson Education. (p.112).

Slowly, students should transit from the story map form to writing a summary in paragraph or continous writing form. For young learners in KG and 1st grade, teachers should teach students that every story has a beginning, middle and an end. A *beginning, middle and end map* is a great method to use when teachers teach young students and can be seen in Figure 2.

Figure 2

Beginning, Middle and End Map

Beginning	**Middle**	**End**
1.	2.	3.

Questioning is another helpful strategy students can use while they read. In this strategy, students develop questions based on what they read. Their questions can be comprised of many different types. The questions can be about the plot of the story, a question about the nature of a character, or a question about a difficult word they may not have understood. Students develop their questions and then read on to discover the answers. Sometimes, students may seek out answers to help improve their comprehension by the use of a dictionary for a difficult word, by the help of another student, or by the help of the teacher.

Students use the strategy of inferring when they draw conclusions about the text based on what they read. For example, if the author of a story states that the sun is shining outside, students can infer that the story takes places during the day. This skill is the most difficult to learn but very important. Teachers should teach this strategy very simply at first, as seen in the above example, and then work up to more complex examples.

Lastly, students should be taught the strategy of visualizing. This strategy is particularly effective with visual learners. Students use the strategy of visualizing when they create pictures in their mind based on what they read.

Comprehension Teaching Methods

Teachers can use Comprehension Teaching Methods to help improve students' comprehension skills. Comprehension teaching methods addressed in this guidebook include: (a) expository text strategies, (b) request procedure, (c) reciprocal teaching, (d) SQ3R, and (e) graphic organizers.

Expository Text is an informational text that, typically, students read in content area classes such as science and social studies. Some expository text strategies include: (a) skim, (b) scan, and (c) GIST (Gipe, 2006). Students skim the text when they quickly go through the material that they will read and note: (a) the title, (b) headings, (c) illustrations, (d) tables, (e) introductions, (f) summaries, and (g) topic sentences. Attention is not focused on any one area, as the goal is to obtain an overall meaning of what they will read. Students scan the text when they look through it quickly, as they search for the answer to a given question. Students use the strategy of GIST when they work in a small group to create a summary statement of a small portion of the text they have read, for example, one paragraph.

Request Procedure (Manzo, 1969, 1985, as cited in Gipe 2006) is where a student and the teacher read a text together and take turns as they practice the comprehension strategy of questioning. The teacher leads by example of how to create appropriate questions and guides the student in the creation of his own questions.

SQ3R (Huber, 2004) is an effective comprehension strategy that students can use to understand both expository and narrative text. SQ3R is an acronym that stands for Survey, Question, Read, Recite, and Review. With SQ3R, the students first survey the material and try to predict what the selection will be about. Then, they develop intelligent questions about what they will read. Next, they read the material, try to recite what they have read, and then bring it all together when they review what they have read.

Graphic Organizers are a great way to help students visualize the organization of text. There are several different types of graphic organizers which include: (a) story maps; (b) charts; (c) webs; (d) grids; (e) matrices; (f) diagrams; (g) cluster maps; (g) beginning, middle, and end maps; (h) description charts; (i) sequence charts; (j) cause and effect charts; (k) KWL charts; and (l) Venn Diagrams. A KWL chart is excellent to use with expository material and can be seen in Figure 3.

Figure 3

KWL Chart

What I Know?	What I Want to Know?	What I Learned?

Vocabulary

Vocabulary is one of the most difficult, and yet, one of the most important concepts in EFL teaching. Most students who seem to struggle with EFL learning, often times, lack sufficient lexical (vocabulary) knowledge. When teachers plan vocabulary lessons for EFL students, they need to provide students with both implicit and explicit learning experiences (Schmitt, 2008). Explicit learning is when teachers directly teach about specific vocabulary words. Implicit learning is when students learn vocabulary through incidental experiences. Also, teachers should teach vocabulary only within contextualized experiences (Beglar & Hunt, 2005; Gersten et al., 2007; Gipe, 2006, Tompkins, 2001). In other words, teachers should choose vocabulary words to teach that come from texts.

There are several different strategies teachers can choose to teach vocabulary. For students, in orderto acquire lexical knowledge through implicit learning, teachers should have students participate in an extensive reading program. Extensive reading is when students read a lot of material that is usually slightly below their actual reading level (Waring, 2009). Typically, students read material at home, and the teacher holds students accountable for their reading by having students complete book reports or by holding personal conferences with each student. Students should read on a daily basis at home and complete one chapter of the book a week in the upper elementary grades. Explicit learning can be accomplished through several different methods some of which include: (a) Gipe's 5-Step Process; (b) talk through; (c) descriptive cues strategy; (d) homophones, homonyms, and homographs; (e) synonym and antonym instruction; (f) semantic word webs; and (g) vocabulary role plays.

Gipe's 5-Step Process

This is a process students can use to understand words in context (Gipe, 2006). The first step involves the use of: (a) context clues, (b) expectancy clues, (c) picture clues, and (d) meaning clues. The students use context clues when they guess word meanings from the context in which the word is found. Expectancy clues are associated with the schemata (background knowledge) that students have in regard to a specific area of study. Picture clues are clues that pictures give in a text. You can see an example of a picture clue in Figure 4.

Figure 4

Picture Clue

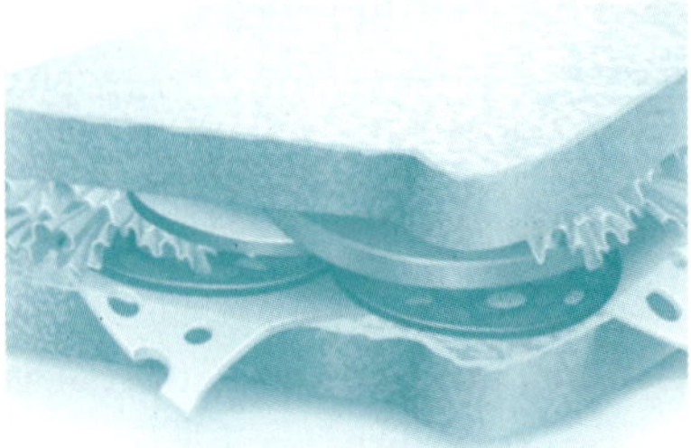

The sandwich looks so tasty!!

Step One: The child is having difficulty decoding the word *sandwich*. He can use picture clues to figure out the word. The teacher can simply point to the picture of the sandwich and then the student will usually get it.

In the second step, Visual Analysis, students break words up into syllables and look at the parts of the words to try and figure out what the words are. In the third step, knowledge of word parts, structural analysis and phonics can be used. Then, in the fourth step, blending and synthesizing can be employed in order to discover a word. Finally, in the fifth step, a dictionary can be consulted to figure out the meaning of a word.

Talk Through

In talk through, first, the teacher writes a sentence on the board with the target word in it and then reads it aloud (Piercey, 1982, as cited in Gipe 2006). Then, she tries to tie the students' background knowledge to the word as she asks questions to the students. Next, she discusses the morphology of the word with the class. Then, she states the meaning of the word and calls on specific students to state an example of how they may have experienced the use of the word in their own lives. Finally, the teacher and the students look again at the original sentence on the board.

Descriptive Cues Strategy

This is a teaching method in which the students are given a worksheet with a small passage on it and are asked to complete four different steps (Gipe, 2006). First, they need to underline the specific word of study in the given passage. Then, they list clues from the passage that help them to identify the meaning of the word. Next, they tie their background knowledge to the word and list any experience that may have helped them to decide what the meaning of the word is. Finally, students write a possible definition of the word. You can see an example of a descriptive cues worksheet in Figure 5.

Figure 5

Descriptive Cues Strategy Worksheet

The excerpt below is taken from *Catwings* by Ursula Le Guin. It is a story about a mother cat, Mrs. Tabby, and her baby kittens who were born with wings.

1. Read the excerpt below. Underline the word *worried* in the excerpt.

2. Find words or phrases in the story that help you understand what the word *worried* means and underline them with a squiggly line.

3. Write about any personal experience you have had in regard to the word *worried.*

----

4. Write a definition for the word *worried* in your own words.

"It's very good, Mother, thank you," they answered happily. They were beautiful children, well brought up. But Mrs. Tabby worried about them secretly. It really was a terrible neighborhood, and getting worse. Car wheels and truck wheels rolling past all day- rubbish and litter- hungry dogs- endless shoes and boots walking, running, stamping, kicking- nowhere safe and quiet, and less and less to eat. Most of the sparrows had moved away. The rats were fierce and dangerous; the mice were shy and scrawny.

Homophones, Homonyms and Homographs

Homophones are words that sound alike but are different in spelling and meaning (Gipe, 2006). Homonyms are words that sound alike and are spelled alike but have different meanings. Homographs are words that are spelled alike but are different in sound and meaning. Such words are highly confusing for EFL students, and teachers should provide direct instruction with these types of words.

Examples:

Homophone: deer (animal) vs. dear (as in writing a letter).

Homonym: row (a line) vs. row (move a boat).

Homograph: bow (as in bow and arrow) vs. bow (as in curtsy).

Try the activity for homophones as shown in Figure 6.

Figure 6

Homophones Activity

Circle the correct homophone of each sentence.

1. The boy pushed the (petals, pedals) to make his bike go.______________
2. My mother uses (flour, flower) to bake a cake. ________________
3. I like to eat my sandwich (plain, plane). ____________________
4. He is not (aloud, allowed) to play outside today. ________________
5. The bobcat circled his (pray, prey) before jumping on him___________

Adapted from: Gipe, J. (2006). *Multiple paths to literacy. Assessment and differentiated instruction for diverse learners,*
K-12. (6th ed.). Upper Saddle River, NJ: Pearson Education (p.112).

Figure 7

Synonym Tree

Adapted from: Gipe, J. (2006). *Multiple paths to literacy. Assessment and differentiated instruction for diverse learners, K-12.* (6th ed.). Upper Saddle River, NJ: Pearson Education (p.263)

Synonym and Antonym Instruction

Synonyms are words that have similar meanings whereas antonyms are words that have opposite meanings. Students can extensively expand their vocabularies with synonym and antonym instruction (Gipe, 2006). Try these activities with students: (a) choose the synonym from a list when an underlined word is used in a sentence, (b) matching activities, (c) circle two different words that would fit in a fill in the blank sentence, (d) fill in the blanks of a small passage where synonyms are listed next to each of the blanks, (e) fill in the blank based on a contextual synonym within the given sentence, and (f) make word webs or word trees for overly used words like *said*. Creative students will enjoy drawing a picture of a tree as they make a synonym tree. At the base of the tree is a word. On the branches are synonyms of the word that is at the base. You can see an example of a synonym tree in Figure 7.

Semantic Word Webs

Teachers can use semantic word webs to help students expand their vocabularies (Tompkins, 2001). There are several different types of word webs. An example of a word web is shown in Figure 8.

Figure 8
Semantic Word Web

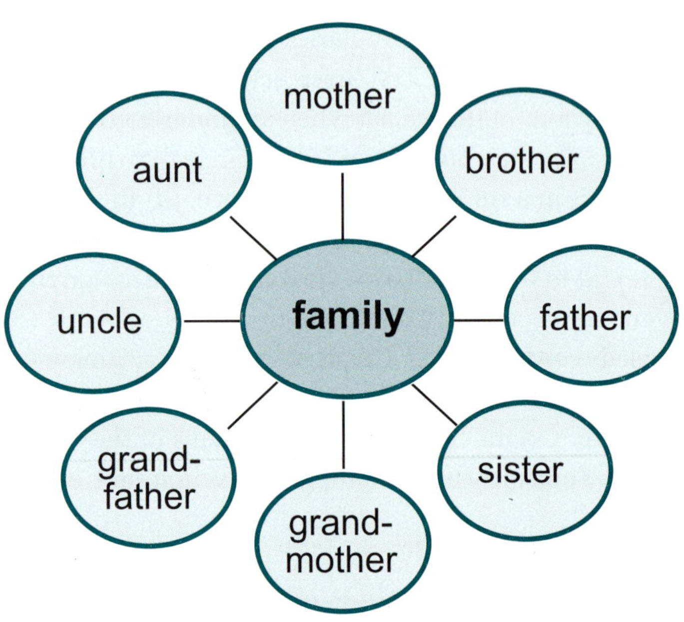

Vocabulary Role Plays

Role plays are a fun and memorable way to teach vocabulary (Gipe, 2006). First, the teacher discusses the word with the class. Then, students create a script using the given vocabulary word. Students then perform the role play for the class. You can see an example of a simple role play for the word *canoeing* in Figure 9. Have fun, use costumes and prepare movements and motions to go with the role plays in order to make the experience a memorable one; and therefore, the students will be more likely to remember the word in question. Although this example is provided to make this concept clear, make sure you let the students create their own role plays.

Figure 9

Role Play for Canoeing

Canoeing

Wise Leader: Jay, you must go down the river and bring us some bread from the people of Chanaqua Valley. It is a long journey, but I'm confident in your **canoeing** skills.

Jay: Yes, my leader, I will do it. I will begin **canoeing** first thing in the morning. I will not let you down.

Narrator: Young Jay set off on his way as he **canoed** down the river to the Chanaqua Valley (Student pantomimes canoeing in the river). When he arrived, the Chanaqua people were very pleased to see him, and immediately helped load his canoe with bread for his village. Young Jay was then on his way home. Unfortunately, the river was rough and tossed his **canoe** side to side (Student should pantomime action).

Jay: Oh No! I don't know if I'm going to make it!!

Narrator: Finally, Jay made it.

Wise Leader: Jay you are a brave soul. You have **canoed** the rough waters and brought food to your people. You will be richly rewarded.

Writing

Writing is an important component of an effective EFL program and should be combined with the reading program as much as possible. Although more time is preferred, due to time constraints in EFL classes today, teachers should devote at least 30 minutes daily to writing, and link the writing activity to the reading of the day. There are several ways to teach writing; however, the writing workshop is the most recommended method. In this guidebook, the following aspects will be addressed: (a) the creation of an effective writing environment, (b) the writing workshop, (c) the writing process, and (d) some different types of writing.

The Creation of An Effective Writing Environment

When teachers set up an EFL writing program, their primary focus needs to be on the creation of an environment that fosters students' creative abilities and removes their inhibitions to help them feel free to compose their own writing. To create such an environment, teachers need to set up the classroom in a motivational, inspirational and functional manner as well as use positive reinforcement and encourage students to use temporary spelling.

The classroom should be well-decorated with learning materials that are bright and uplifting, as well as useful. Some ideas include: (a) a chart of grammar mini lessons learned in the class; (b) a bulletin board of the whole class story for the week with students' compositions about the story; (c) KG and 1st grade classrooms can display opening routine bulletin boards of the calendar, weather, numbers, colors, letters, nursery rhymes, etc; (d) the writing process chart; (e) synonym, antonym, homophone, homonym, and homograph charts; (f) inspirational charts that encourage students to write; and (g) a writing bulletin board that changes monthly based on different themes to inspire ideas for writing. You can see Figure 10 for an example of a fantasy writing bulletin board where the small squares represent areas to post students' fantasy stories that they create themselves.

The classroom should also be set up in a functional manner that encourages students to write. In KG and 1st grade classrooms in particular, teachers should provide writing centers that are stocked with several different materials which include: (a) pens, markers, crayons, pencils; (b) papers of different sizes, colors, with lines and blank pages; (c) glue, glitter, yarn, material scraps; and (d) readymade booklets students can use to make their own books. Young students will find all of these materials a lot of fun and will be encouraged to write their own stories, letters, and books. Although older students also find the above materials motivating, many older students are more encouraged through actual exposure to reading and books. Therefore, it is important to maintain a fully stocked classroom library that students have access to on a daily basis in all grade levels. It is recommended that classroom libraries contain approximately five to eight books per student (Morrow, 2005).

Finally, teachers can create an effective writing environment by the use of positive reinforcement and the encouragement of temporary spelling. Teachers' number one priority should be to encourage students to be creative and get their ideas down on paper. Content is the first step of writing and the most important. A good way to help improve a students' content is by asking the questions that will encourage the student to add detail to his or her composition. Another way to help improve students' content is to encourage students to use temporary spelling. A detailed description of what temporary spelling is can be seen in the spelling section later in this chapter. Teachers should always be very positive when consulting with their students in regard to their students' writing. When a teacher wants a student to improve his or her paper, she should begin her response with a positive comment, and then offer a suggestion for improvement.

Figure 10
Fantasy Writing Bulletin Board

The Writing Workshop

The writing workshop is a separate time period in which students focus only on their writing. The workshop consists of three different parts: (a) writing, (b) sharing, and (c) mini lesson (Tompkins, 2001). Usually, workshops begin with a small mini lesson that directly appeals to the majority of the students' needs and range in topics from phonics instruction to content development. After the mini lesson, students are given time to write independently. Towards the end of the workshop, students share their compositions with other students and the teacher. During the workshop, the teacher circulates around the room as she works individually with students and emphasizes the use of the writing process.

Typically, it is preferred for students to choose their own purposes for writing and topics to write on; however, the teacher may need to offer some suggestions to get kids on the right track. Occasionally, a teacher may choose a type of writing that students should be required to write about. In younger grades, teachers need to offer a lot of direction and often, most students will be working at the same pace. In grade 2 and above, students start to vary their writing and tend to be at different stages of the writing process. In these grade levels, it is important to give students time if they require it. Some students may need two to three class periods to compose their first drafts, whereas other students may compose their first draft in one class period, but spend two to three class periods in the revision and editing stages. A true writing workshop lets students work at their own pace, as long as they are productively working.

Starting in grade 3, a teacher may want to make a list of different types of writing projects that students are required to write during the year, and let each student work at their own pace to accomplish the given projects. See Figure 11 for a 3rd grade chart you can post in class to remind students of the required writing projects for the school year. Remember, the teacher will need to provide direct instruction on how to complete each of the required writing projects.

Figure 11

3rd Grade Required Writings for the Year

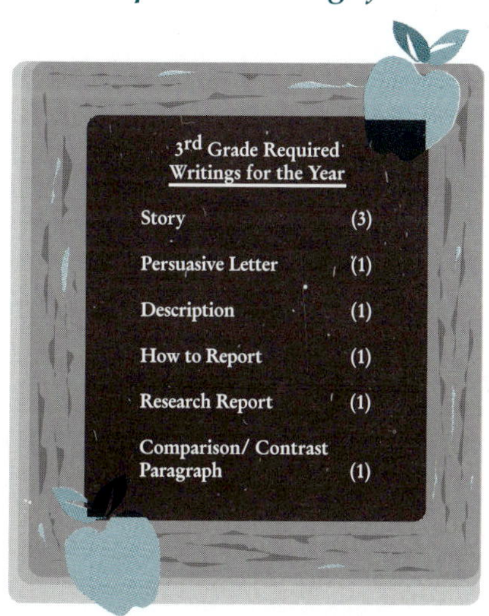

In Appendix A–Daily Lesson Plans, you can see an example of how to conduct a writing workshop in a 1st grade classroom. On Tuesday, the workshop begins with an explanation of how the students will write their own descriptions of their favorite sea creature. Before students begin individual work, they first learn about capitalization in a mini lesson. Students are then free to work individually as the teacher circulates around the class and asks students questions about the content of their papers. On Wednesday, the teacher begins the writing workshop with a mini lesson on editing. Students are then free to edit and revise their papers independently as the teacher circulates around the room helping students. On Thursday, students complete their descriptions and share their finished compositions with the class. In many classrooms, teachers use a writing workshop daily, especially in grades 4 and above. However, in the example provided in Appendix A of a 1st grade classroom, the writing workshop is combined with two whole class writing activities.

The Writing Process

The writing process is a five step process that students follow when they develop their own compositions (Gipe, 2006: Morrow, 2005; Tompkins, 2001). This process includes: (a) prewriting, (b) drafting, (c) revising, (d) editing, and (e) publishing. Each phase is important and needs to be explicitly taught to the students. Prewriting is when students write their ideas on paper and it includes such activities as: (a) drawing, (b) drama enactments, or (c) speed writing. Drafting is when students write the first draft of their composition based on their prewriting activities. Next, in revision, students try to expand, elaborate and fix up the content of their compositions. Then, students focus on the mechanics of grammar and spelling in the editing phase. Finally, students publish their work and share it with others, such as classmates, the teacher, the principal, or parents. When teachers teach students how to use the writing process, they ensure that students will become proficient writers.

Prewriting is the first step in the writing process and critical in content development. To help 1st graders get started, drawing is an excellent prewriting activity. Students can use the *beginning, middle, and end map*, as shown in Figure 2, to create their own story and use as a prewriting activity. First, students draw a picture for the beginning of the story. Then, they draw pictures for the middle and end of the story. After drawing the pictures, they can then write the 1st draft of their story.

Types of Writing

Teachers can choose from several different types of writing when they instruct students on how to write; however, we will address: (a) small group collaborative writing, (b) interactive writing, (c) the language experience approach, and (d) creative writing.

Small Group Collaborative Writing is when students work with each other and/or the teacher to create compositions (Gipe, 2006). If a teacher has chosen a guided reading approach with small groups as her reading instruction program, then one type of center to include in this reading period would be a small group collaborative writing center. In a collaborative writing center, students work independently in a small group of 5-6 students. Usually, the teacher gives the group a topic and then makes them create a small story on a large chart paper together as a group. Each student can contribute one sentence to the story and sign his or her name next to his or her sentence. Later, their story chart is displayed in the class and can be shared with other students and the teacher.

Interactive Writing is another popular method of writing for primary students. In interactive writing, the teacher creates a small story on the board with the help of the students (Soderman et al., 2005). In the beginning, the teacher starts the story and models appropriate writing. After some time, students begin to contribute their own ideas as well. Throughout this process, the teacher consistently brings to attention key concepts she wants the students to learn, for example, capitalization, punctuation, etc. You can see an example of interactive writing in Appendix A–Monday writing block.

Another type of writing very similar to interactive writing is the **Language Experience Approach**. In the language experience approach, students recall information from actual experiences they have had and then create a composition, with the help of the teacher, in the same manner as interactive writing (Morrow, 2005). However, with the language experience approach, the teacher first writes whatever the students dictate and then, after they complete the story, the teacher goes back and discusses with the students how they can improve their story as they change content, punctuation, capitalization, etc. You can see an example of the lesson that uses the language experience approach in Appendix A–Friday writing block.

Finally, **Creative Writing** is when students make their own compositions based on their own ideas and experiences (Gipe, 2006). Students can make up a story, write a recipe, write a letter to a friend, etc. The best thing about creative writing is that it allows students to use their minds and employ critical thinking skills that are necessary as students grow older. Many students will be hesitant at first to write and will have difficulty coming up with their own ideas. Often times, a casual conversation with the teacher about a student's interests can often spark new ideas and inspire students to write. Students can also keep idea notebooks,in which they jot down ideas for writing topics as they think of them to be used later during the writing workshop. See Table 9 for Creative Writing Ideas for 4th to 6th grade classrooms.

Table 9

Creative Writing Prompts for 4th to 6th grade classrooms

Creative Writing Prompts
❖ When Sharon opened the door of the closet, she could not see her clothes, but a beautiful forest.
❖ The whole family sat down for the picnic, and thebear sat down with them.
❖ Write 200 words on the life of a mosquito.
❖ A beggar has won a million dollars in a lottery. Write about the thoughts that emerge inside his mind and the behavior of the people around him before he goes and takes the money.
❖ A group of students stumble upon a cave when they drift off from the other students while on a picnic in the forest.
❖ Write a story that includes this sentence: "This pendant is the only way that you can enter the castle."
❖ A spaceship stumbles onto a planet full of aliens that look like flowers.
❖ The new house owner discovers an old photograph in the attic.
❖ Gretchen has lied to save her friend from trouble. Now she is in more trouble because she has to keep lying to continue the story that she has told. When will her troubles end?
❖ A random cleaning up of the house leads to the discovery of an old diary.

Information Source: Ghare, M. (2007). Creative writing prompts. *Buzzle.com website.* Retrieved May 10, 2009, from http://www.buzzle.com/articles/creative-writing-prompts.html

Grammar

Grammar is often seen as a huge problem that teachers need to overcome with their students. Many teachers receive written compositions full of grammar errors and are unsure of how they should approach the correction of their students' papers. Often, many teachers spend countless hours as they correct grammar on students' papers and become highly frustrated when they have to correct the same types of errors in future compositions. Grammar correction **DOES NOT WORK** (Krashen, 1999, as cited in Muncie, 2002). Instead of correcting the endless grammatical mistakes in students' papers, teachers should give specific instruction about common grammatical problems that students experience in their writing. Grammar instruction should serve a functional purpose (Kotapish, 1993). In other words, teach grammar concepts that directly affect students' speaking or writing ability. Grammar is an important component of any EFL program, but it needs to be taught in an appropriate manner in order to best serve EFL students. The following guidelines should be used when teachers prepare grammar curriculum:

- First, assess students' writing and oral language to determine common grammatical problems.

- Second, choose a common grammatical problem observed in assessment and conduct a mini-lesson (Gray, 2004) to show students the proper use of language in regard to the given grammatical problem. An example of a grammar mini-lesson on the present continuous tense can be seen in Appendix A.

- Third, have students find and correct mistakes in regard to the specific grammatical problem as taught in the mini-lesson in their own compositions.

- Fourth, make a poster of the grammar mini-lessons that have been taught in class and have students refer to it often when they write compositions.

- Fifth, do not correct students' grammatical errors on their papers. This type of correction is ineffective and often discourages students from producing creative and ambitious writing projects, as they are afraid to receive their paper back full of red marks.

- Sixth, if parents and school administration require students to write grammatically perfect papers, then error correction should only be utilized in the last stage of the writing process, i.e. the editing stage (Hedge, 1988; Ferris, 1999, both cited in Muncie, 2002).

Spelling

Spelling is an important aspect of EFL teaching as many people see students who are proficient at spelling as more capable and intelligent than other students who do not spell as well. Particularly in Pakistan, this is true. However, several researchers (Bear, Invernizzi, Templeton, & Johnston, 1996; Gipe, 2006; Lundblade, 1994; Morrow, 2005; Soderman, Gregory, & McCarty, 2005; Tompkins, 2001) have shown support for the use of temporary spelling, as it allows students to experiment with writing and builds their confidence as writers since they are better able to communicate their message. Temporary spelling is defined as the manner in which students apply developmentally appropriate phonetic skills learned when they try to spell words. For example, a beginning speller may spell the word "*cat*" as such "*ct*". Students who are limited to the use of those words, which they have memorized, do not tend to enjoy writing or produce as high quality ideas as students who can use temporary spelling. When students first learn how to write, it is important that teachers focus more on the content and ideas of their papers than on spelling each word correctly. The following guidelines should be used when teachers develop spelling curriculum for EFL students:

- Allow students to use temporary spelling in order to help

them express their ideas more fully.

- Have students correct their spelling errors in the editing phase of the writing process.

- Transition students to conventional spelling by the use of explicit spelling instruction.

- Focus on a minimum amount of words weekly (e.g. 10 words for 1st class) in which students are expected to spell the given words correctly on a weekly spelling test.

- Choose sight words and high frequency words as the weekly spelling words. In higher grade levels (4th, 5th, 6th), choose commonly misspelled words as well as words that students will encounter in their reading program.

Spelling Ideas

Personal Dictionaries: (Gipe, 2006) Have students create their own A to Z dictionaries in which they can add new words as they learn them. Dictionaries are quite useful for students to refer to during writing time.

Word Making: (Tompkins, 2001) Students make words from letter cards. A *c* card and an *at* card together make the word cat.

Word Sorts: Students sort words into different categories, e.g. vehicles with two wheels and vehicles with more than two wheels.

Spelling Collages: (Morrow, 2005) Students create a collage by cutting out letters to make their weekly spelling words.

Word Walls: (Tompkins, 2001) Create a wall of words for students to refer to when they write. A high frequency word wall of the 100 most frequent words is great for a 1st grade classroom.

Cheerleader Spelling: (Gipe, 2006) Students spell words with movements. They stand up with hands up for letters that reach the top line e.g. *h*, they stand with hands down for letters on the bottom line only e.g. *c*, and they squat for letters that go below the bottom line, e.g. *y*.

Word Searches: Students search for spelling words in a word search.

Trace a Word: (Morrow, 2005) Students trace their spelling words with several colors. Great for KG and 1st grade.

Oral Language

Oral language is made up of two essential language skills of listening and speaking and is of high priority in every EFL classroom. In Pakistan, often, students have to face the difficult challenge of English language testing when they take the International English Language Testing System (IELTS) test or the Test of English as a Foreign Language (TOEFL). In both of these examinations, students have to complete sections in both speaking and listening. Students must receive satisfactory marks on one of these two examinations in order to study abroad in universities all over the world. Preparation for these exams begins when students first start to learn English. With this in mind, educators in Pakistan need to focus on oral language on a daily basis. There are many different types of activities teachers can choose from to develop students' oral skills; however, we will address: (a) oral skills with beginning learners; (b) task-based learning; and (c) drama and role plays.

Oral Skills with Beginning Learners

Working with beginning learners can be extremely challenging, as often, beginning learners have a vocabulary of only two to three words of English. This presents quite a problem as teachers will have much difficulty if they adopt an *only English* philosophy in their classroom, where teachers only speak in the English language. In Pakistan, students usually begin English instruction at the age of 4-5 (British Council, 2004). Typically, this is in the nursery class, one class before kindergarten (Prep). When teachers work with nursery class students, they need to employ use of the students' native language in order to aid students' comprehension. Teachers should limit their native language use in prep class and completely eliminate its use in classes 1 and above, unless absolutely necessary. Also, teachers should use visual aids to represent words as much as possible. One great technique to use with young learners is the use of repetition with basic communication phrases as well as the use of simple questions and answers. Teachers should choose very simple, common phrases and have students learn them slowly one at time. Learning one to two small phrases a week is most appropriate for nursery class students. Teachers can begin this type of instruction at times most suitable for certain phrases. For example, when students first enter into the class in the morning, they should be taught to say, "Hello, how are you?" Students can also learn phrases such as "Can you open this?", "May I go and play?" or "This is really good."

Task-Based Learning

Task-based learning is where students use the target language (English) in order to accomplish a given task (Willis, 1996, as cited in Asato, 2003). There are several different types of tasks which include: (a) order and sort, (b) compare, (c) problem solve, (d) share personal experiences, (e) creative tasks, and (f) listing. When students complete task-based learning activities, it is important that the teacher emphasizes that the students are only allowed to use English during the process. Teachers should actively monitor the process to ensure students speak in English only. One way to ensure that the students use only English during activities is to teach students phrases of negotiation such as *Can you repeat that?* or *Are you ready?*, as students tend to employ the use of their native language most often when they try to move the task along in order to accomplish their goal. In Table 10, you can see several different ideas of task based learning activities.

Table 10

Task-Based Learning Ideas

Order and Sort	Compare	Problem Solving	Share Personal Experiences	Creative Tasks	Listing
Students discuss the steps of how to ride a bike	Students compare two different cities	Students create a plan to get kids off the streets working and into school	Students discuss how they spent their summer vacation	Students work together to create a kite	Students make a list of words that start with P
Students sort means of transportation into different groups	Students compare dogs and cats	Students plan a school function	Students discuss what happened when they misbehaved	Students work together to create a role play	Students make a list of different occupations
Students discuss the steps of how to fly a kite	Students compare two different amusement parks	Students plan and conduct a speech contest	Students discuss their favorite hobby	Students build a ship made from ice cream sticks	Students make a list of favorite stories read

Drama and Role Plays

The use of drama in the classroom with scripted dialogues allows students to easily acquire the vocabulary, idioms, grammar and syntax of English speech (Berlinger, 2000, as cited in Boucher & Leong, 2002). Also, the use of drama can be highly motivational and memorable for many students. Teachers may use prepared scripts in which students memorize their lines and then perform for an audience, or a more casual approach, such as readers' theater may be used. When students use scripted dialogues, they create sets, use props, practice movements and memorize lines as they prepare for their performance. With readers' theater, students can read their parts from a script, as they practice their intonation and phrasing. Very few props are used in readers' theater; however, students repeatedly practice their lines as they prepare for a performance as well. Teachers can use prepared scripts or they may have students create their own scripts. Also, students can create readers' theater scripts from popular stories they have read in class.

Appropriate Error Correction

It can be challenging to teach EFL students, as beginning students tend to make many mistakes, and teachers may be confused about how they should approach the error correction process with their students. Based on researched practices, it is best to do minimal error correction in the EFL classroom (Asato, 2003; Gersten et. al., 2007; Peinemann, 1995). Teachers' priority focus should be on the establishment of an environment which motivates students and encourages them to take risks with newly learned language skills. When teachers correct students repeatedly, students become apprehensive and hesitant to speak in the class for fear of being embarrassed. Teachers should do selective error correction in a positive manner that affirms the students' knowledge. Teachers should not correct every error, but only specific errors that the teacher wants the students to learn.

- First, orally assess students to see what type of mistakes they are making. Mistakes can range from improper use of tenses to subject-verb agreement errors. The focus here should be on grammatical errors.

- Second, choose one concept at a time to reinforce with error correction.

- Third, ignore all errors except for the specific areas you have decided to have the students learn.

- Fourth, perform error correction in a positive manner that affirms student's knowledge and motivates him to take further risks. In the example below, the teacher has given Billy positive reinforcement as he has answered the question correctly by stating it was the body who rides the bike, however, his grammar is incorrect. To help Billy learn the correct grammar, she simply restates his answer correctly. In this manner, Billy still feels good that he got the correct answer, and he hears the appropriate way to say the sentence.

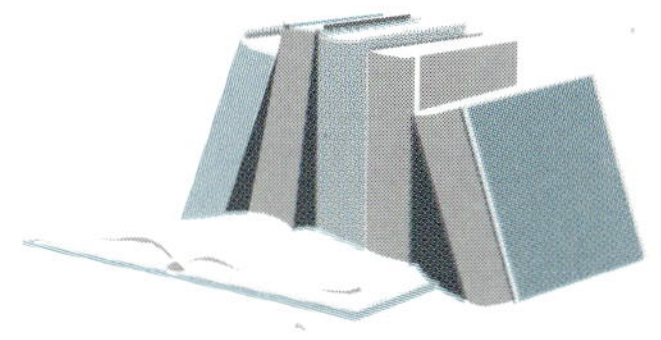

Week at a Glance in a 1st Grade Classroom

As teachers begin to plan instruction based on this guidebook, they may feel a bit overwhelmed and unsure of how to fit everything together. To help ease teachers into this style of teaching, a sample weekly planner and daily lesson plans are provided. The weekly planner is a quick reference tool that teachers can glance at during class time to remind themselves what lessons to teach. The daily lesson plans give more detailed information on how to teach each lesson and can be found in Appendix A.

In this week-long plan, a combined approach of whole class reading instruction and small group instruction is used. Although there will be 4-6 different reading groups in the class, instruction is shown for only one group. Keep in mind that instruction for small groups needs to be planned according to the students' ability levels and literacy needs. In Table 11, you can see the weekly planner for the Reading Block and in Table 12, you can see the weekly planner for the Writing Block.

This week-long plan uses the *New Oxford Modern English* student textbook (Horsburgh, 2009) and two short stories from the *Oxford Literacy Web: Hermit Crab's New Shell* (Moon, 1999) and *Shark's Tooth* (Moon, 1999). The student textbook is divided into 21 units and it is recommended that teachers spend approximately two weeks on each unit. Some of the smaller units should be completed in one week. Teachers should supplement this program with other children's literature. The week long plan supplements the student's textbook with two short stories; one small story is used for whole class reading instruction and the other story is used with one of the small reading groups. The students in each small group should be reading different stories according to their ability level.

Table 11

Weekly Reading Planner

Weekly Planner of a 1st Grade Classroom

60-Minute Reading Time Block

Monday	Vocabulary: NO, p.11 15 min	Read Aloud NO Outside and Inside p.11 8 min Reading Groups 10 min	Spelling- Intro new words and write in copies. 22 min	Oral language Discuss what people do outside and inside 5 min
Tuesday	Preview and predict Hermit Crab's New Shell, teach and do beginning, middle, and end maps 45 min	Oral Language: Have students orally make sentences with spelling words. 15 min		
Wednesday	Vocabulary for Hermit Crab 15 min	Finish beginning, middle, and end maps 10 min Reading groups 10 min	Oral Language Task-based learning: Students make a list of things found in the sea 15 min	Play spelling make a word game 10 min
Thursday	Reading groups 25 min	Grammar mini lesson on present continuous tense 20 min	Oral language Talk about your favorite sea creature 15 min	
Friday	Comprehension of NO Outside and Inside p.13 A, 2 Fill in the blanks 10 min	Comprehension of Hermit the Crab, Make crab tissue charts/ and assessment 25 min	Spelling Test 15 min	Oral Language NO, p. 13 Questions and answers orally 10 min

NO= New Oxford Modern English student textbook

Table 12

Weekly Writing Planner

Weekly Planner of a 1st Grade Classroom

30-Minute Writing Time Block

Monday	Whole group Interactive Writing Story about a sea creature.
Tuesday	Write about your favorite sea creature at least 4 sentences. Mini lesson on capitalization.
Wednesday	Continue story about sea creature. Mini lesson on editing.
Thursday	Finish story about sea creature. Create pictures to go with story.
Friday	Language Experience Approach Story about going to the beach.

APPENDICES

Appendix A

Daily Lesson Plans

Monday

Reading Block: Reading, Spelling, Vocabulary, Oral language (60 min).

Vocabulary: *New Oxford*, p.11 (15 min).

Objective: Students will learn new words and will be able to point them out on the white board when the teacher asks about specific vocabulary words as well as match pictures to the corresponding vocabulary word.

1. Write the following words on the board and say them aloud: basket, bowl, mending, painting, shopping, stove. Ask students which words they are familiar with and what experiences they may have had with the words. Example, a student may say they have cooked spaghetti before on a stove.

2. Say each word and have the class repeat the word after you. Show actual objects when you say the words basket, bowl, and stove (use a play stove).Use a pantomime procedure or pictures to demonstrate the words mending, painting, and shopping.
3. Ask students to pantomime painting and mending with hand motions.
4. Ask one student to be a shopkeeper and another to be a customer. Tell them to demonstrate how someone goes shopping. Encourage them to use words.
5. Ask different students to come up to the board and point to the correct vocabulary word you state, as well as to either point to the object or pantomime the word you say. For example, if you say *basket*, the student should point to the word *basket* on the board and then point to the actual object(basket) as well. If there is time, you can also have students complete the vocabulary assessment worksheet at the end of this day's lesson plan.

Reading: Read aloud NO *Outside and Inside* p. 11 (8 min). Reading groups (10 min)

Objective: Students will begin to improve their comprehension by listening to a story.Students will be able to read the story *Shark's Tooth.*

1. Read aloud the story *Outside and Inside* on p. 11 (8 min).
2. Small Reading Groups: Students should be made to sit in small groups with no more than 6 students in any group. Instruction is shown for only one group; however, the teacher will need to plan instruction for all groups and move around each group to give them instruction. (10 min)

a. Students should be able to read all words in the story by themselves by the end of the week. Students should not advance on to the next story until they have mastered all the words in their current story. Some stories may require more than one week for the students to learn.

b. Teachers should communicate regularly with parents, so parents understand the goals of the reading program.

c. Students will begin learning to read through memorization of stories. This is natural and the beginning steps of reading. Have students point to each word as they read, so they start to learn to recognize the words instead of memorizing whole sentences without really knowing the words.

d. During reading group time, you should have a teacher's aid and possibly parent helpers in the class to work with the other reading groups in the same manner as the teacher. The teacher should move to the other groups on a regular basis so she can monitor and assess students' learning. If helpers are unavailable, the teacher will need to plan literacy activities for the other groups to do as she works with one group.

- Show the cover of *Shark's Tooth* to the group. Ask them what they think the story will be about.
- Picture walk the story, as you show each page ask for students' responses about what they think is happening in the story without reading the text. Read the story aloud to the students. Discuss with the students what happened in the beginning, middle, and end of the story.

Spelling: Introduce new words and write them in copies (22min).

Objective: Students will learn how to spell new words and spell them correctly on a spelling test.

1. Write all the spelling words on the board and ask different students if they can read them. Spelling words: mother, of, out, clap, clip, slam, slap, chip, drop, drip.
2. Say each of the spelling words and have the class repeat them after you. Point out the words *mother, of, out* on the high frequency word wall. Ask different students to state a sentence orally with each word. Clarify any misunderstandings and provide examples, if necessary.
3. Write the blends *cl, sl, ch*, and *dr* one at a time on the top of the white board. Ask students if they know what sound each blend makes. Have students repeat the sound a few times after you for each blend. Write *claw, slip, chat*, and *drape* under the corresponding blend when discussing its sound. Have students repeat the blend sound and the word for each one.
4. Ask students to arrange the phonic spelling words: *clap, clip, slam, slap, ship, drop, drip* under the correct blend on the board. Teachers may choose one student at a time to come to the board and place one spelling word under the correct blend.
5. Have students write all 10 spelling words in their copy as you say them. Keep the spelling words on the board for students to refer to, but encourage them to try and write the word first, and then check the board to see if they are correct.

Oral Language: Discuss what people do outside and inside (5 min).

Objective: Students will learn new vocabulary and improve their speaking skills by participating in oral language activities.

1. Ask students, "Are we inside the classroom or outside the classroom?" Explain to students that there are many things we can do when we are inside.

2. Tell them that,“I can teach students when I’m inside.” Ask students what type of things they can do when they are inside. Encourage students to speak in complete sentences. Use appropriate error correction as indicated in the guidebook. List the activities they do on the board under the word inside. Repeat the above procedure for the word outside.

Writing Block: Whole group interactive writing, story about a sea creature (30 min).

Objective: Students will contribute to a group story with the teacher.

1. Ask students what type of sea creatures they know about. Discuss the different animals.
2. The teacher creates a story about one of the animals discussed with the students. The teacher should begin the story and note how she begins the first sentence with a capital letter and ends it with a period as she writes it on the whiteboard. The teacher should also point out any high frequency words used that have already been learned in class as well as spelling words. The teacher should ask the students to help her spell certain words, especially words that use the week’s phonic concept of blends, i.e. *sl*, *ch*, *dr*, and *cl*.
3. The teacher asks students what they think the animal should do in the story and takes their ideas. She should then create appropriate gramatically correct sentences. Gradually, the teacher should start to use sentences as given by the students if they are grammatically accurate. If not, she should first correct them before writing them on the whiteboard. Make sure to use appropriate error correction guidelines.
4. Make sure to guide students in the creation of a story with a beginning, middle, and end.
5. After completing the story, ask a few students to read the story aloud to the class.

Name: ____________ Date: ____________

Outside and Inside Vocabulary Assessment

Match the word with the correct picture.

1. **basket**

2. **bowl**

3. **mending**

4. **painting**

5. **shopping**

6. **stove**

Tuesday

Reading Block: Reading, Oral language (60 min).

Reading: Preview and predict *Hermit Crab's New Shell.* Teach and complete beginning, middle and end maps (45 min).

> *Objective:* Students will learn that stories have a beginning, middle and end. Students will understand the story *Hermit Crab's New Shell* and complete an extension activity to reinforce their learning.

1. Ask students if they have ever been to the sea before. Briefly discuss their experiences.
2. Show students the cover of *Hermit Crab's New Shell.* Ask students what they think the story will be about. Discuss. Read the story aloud to the students and confirm if their predictions were correct or not.
3. Ask students what happened in the beginning of the story (Hermit crab doesn't like his shell and leaves to find another one). You can use the pictures in the book to help remind students what happened. Ask students what happened in the middle of the story (for example Hermit crab finds a pretty spotted shell, but there was someone inside). Ask students what happened at the end of the story (Hermit crab finds a nice shell he really likes and then discovers it's his own original shell). During this discussion, the teacher can use an overhead projector and fill out the beginning, middle, and end map. The teacher should demonstrate how to draw a picture to go with each section and how the text should go below its picture.
4. Now give each student a map of his or her own. Students should fill it out themselves with their own responses. Make sure to remove the example you had done previously on the overhead so students do not just copy your example. It is good to have students create their own sentences themselves.

Oral Language: Have students orally make sentences with spelling words (15 min).

Objective: Students will learn new vocabulary and improve their speaking skills by participating in oral language activities.

1. Make groups of 5-6 students and ask them to create sentences for two different spelling words.
2. Groups can then present their sentences to the rest of the class by writing them on the board and reading them aloud.

Writing Block: Write about your favorite sea creature, mini-lesson on capitalization (30 min).

Objective: Students will create their own descriptions of at least 4 sentences.
Descriptions should demonstrate appropriate capitalization.

1. Ask students if they remember the story we wrote yesterday. Ask students to recall what happened in the story.
2. Ask students what their favorite sea creatures are. Write the names of the sea creatures on the white board.
3. Tell students they need to choose one sea creature as their favorite and write a paragraph of at least 4 sentences to describe it. Write the following excerpt on the board and read it aloud to the class to serve as an example. When writing, point out to students how to use a capital letter at the beginning of each sentence.

Eel

My favorite sea creature is an eel.
I think eels are really cool because they are
long and slimy. An eel swims in the sea.
Most eels are black and grey.

4. Have students work independently to create their own sea creature descriptions. Leave the example and names of creatures on the board for students to refer to. Tell students they cannot copy the example; they need to make their own sentences.
5. The teacher should take rounds of the classroom and help students. Encourage students to use temporary spelling and tell students to spell the words as best they can. Do not give spellings on the first day. The teacher should reinforce the mini-lesson on capitalization as she consults with students.

Wednesday

Reading Block: Vocabulary, Reading, Oral language, Spelling (60 min).

Vocabulary: for *Hermit the Crab* (15 min).

Objective: Students will learn new words and will be able to point them out when the teacher asks a question about a specific vocabulary word.

1. Ask students to recall the story they had read about the crab. Ask them where did the crab live? Discuss where he lived and show the picture on page 2 of the old broken boat under the sea.
2. Read page 3 aloud to the class. *Hermit Crab lived in the old wreck.* Ask students what they think the word wreck means? Discuss and clarify their responses. A wreck is a broken down object, it can refer to a broken vehicle,

boat, crashed vehicles or even a human being, i.e. *She looks like a wreck.*

3. Make a semantic word web on the white board using the word wreck in the middle. Ask students if they can think of other words that can be used instead of the word wreck. Students should give responses such as: broken boat, broken house, beat up car, tired and untidy person, cars that have crashed, etc.
4. Show students the cover of the *Hermit Crab's New Shell.* Write "Hermit Crab" on the board. Explain to students that a hermit crab is a specific kind of crab that lives inside a shell in the sea. Show page 5 where you can see the Hermit Crab outside his shell and discuss that he has 4 legs and two pinching arms just like other crabs, but hermit crabs live inside of shells. Show page 16 of the story where you see the Hermit Crab back inside of his shell.
5. Point to the Hermit crab's shell and explain to students that we call this a shell. Show an actual shell that students can see. Write the word "shell" on the board and ask students to repeat the word after you.
6. Write the word "inside" on the board. Ask students where does the Hermit crab live? They should respond *inside the shell.* Tell them that this is the word inside as you point the word out on the board. Ask them to tell you what objects you have placed inside of a small box. Have an apple and pen inside a box for students to see.
7. Write the word "spotted" on the board. Tell students this is the word spotted. Take a dry erase marker and make spots on your face. Ask students to describe what your face looks like. Students should say you have *a spotted face.* Also, show students a spotted stuffed animal and explain that the animal is also spotted.
8. Write *hermit crab, wreck, shell, spotted* and *inside* on the board. Call on different students to come to the board and point to the correct word that answers the given question.

a. The hermit crab lives inside of what?
b. Where is the apple?
c. What kind of stuffed animal do we have in class today?
d. These sea creatures like to live inside of shells.
e. The broken down car was such a ______________.

9. For extra practice, have students complete the following worksheet for homework.

Reading: Finish beginning, middle, and end maps (10 min).
Reading Groups (10 min).

Objective: Students will learn that stories have a beginning, middle and end. Students will understand the story *Hermit Crab's New Shell* and complete an extension activity to reinforce their learning. Students learn how to read the story *Shark's Tooth.*

1. Students work to complete their beginning, middle, and end maps that they had started yesterday.
2. Reading groups: read (Echo Reading) the text, *Shark's Tooth.*

- You say one sentence, or part of a sentence, if the sentence is too long for the students to remember, and then students repeat it after you. Make sure to use proper intonation and phrasing to serve as an example for the students.
- Do the same for the whole story. Work individually with some students as you do echo reading with them, and have other students try to read the text by themselves.

Hermit Crab's New Shell Vocabulary Homework

Name: ____________________ Date: ____________________

Class: ____________________

Draw a line to match the correct picture with the correct word.

1. shell

2. hermit crab

3. spotted

4. wreck

5. inside

Oral language: Task-based learning.

Students make a list of things found in the sea. (15 min).

Objective: Students will learn new vocabulary and improve their speaking skills by participating in oral language activities.

1. Mack groups of 5-6 students and ask them to create a list of things found in the sea. Make a competition between the groups.
2. Groups present their list orally to the rest of the class. Whichever group has the most correct words can be awarded with a prize, such as allowing them to leave five minutes early for the break time.

Spelling: Play "spelling makes a word" game (10 min).

Objective: Students will learn how to spell new words and spell them correctly on a spelling test.

1. Pair students up and give them a set of cards in order to play a spelling game. There should be 2 *cl* cards, 2 *sl* cards, 1 *ch* card, 2 *dr* cards, 2 *ap* cards, 3 *ip* cards, 1 *am* card, and 1 *op* card.
2. Students work in pairs together to form their spelling words.

Writing Block: Continue story on a sea creature. Mini lesson on editing (30 min).

Objective: Students will create their own descriptions. Students will learn how to edit capitalization and punctuation and edit their own papers.

1. Students continue to work on the sea creature descriptions. Some students may complete their first draft and now need to move on to the revision and editing stage.
2. Explain to students that after you write something, you go back and try to find mistakes and fix them. This is called editing.
3. Write the following sentence on the board and ask students to help you fix it. They should point out that it needs a capital letter, a period (.) and *is* needs to be added before the word *swimming*.

the sea horse swimming in the sea

4. Tell students we edited the above sentence and they need to edit their papers in the same manner. Tell students to find sentences that need capital letters. Let students work individually to edit their papers. The teacher should take rounds of the class to help students individually.

Thursday

Reading Block: Reading, grammar, oral language (60 min).
Reading: Reading Groups

Objective: Students will learn how to read the story *Shark's Tooth*.

1. Choral read the text, *Shark's Tooth,* with the small group. The teacher and students read the text at the same time together.
2. Have students read the text again by themselves and then complete a beginning, middle, and end map of the story.
3. As students work independently, work with one student in the small group at a time as you do guided reading

with him or her. He or she reads the story on his own as you help only when needed. Encourage the student to use many different reading strategies to figure out unknown words. Do not automatically help when the student is stuck on a word.

Grammar: Mini lesson on present continuous tense (20 min).

Objective: Students will demonstrate proper use of the present continuous tense by answering questions correctly and writing the correct tense verb in the fill in the blank.

1. Ask students to recall the story *Outside and Inside* that was read previously in class. Ask students to name some of the people who were in the story.

2. Ask students to raise their hand to tell you what Abdul is doing on page 11 of their *New Oxford Modern English* Textbook. Call on one student to answer the question. Choose an average student that may struggle stating the answer with appropriate grammar, but loves to volunteer answers in class. Make sure to offer positive reinforcement for the effort the student gives in answering the question, whether or not the correct answer has been given. Possible teacher response:
"*Good try, right. Abdul is painting the gate.*"

3. Write the sentence "*Abdul is painting the gate.*" on the board. Ask the students if Abdul painted the gate yesterday. They should respond no, if not, give them the answer. Ask students *"Will Abdul paint the gate tomorrow?"* Students should respond no. Ask students when did Abdul paint the gate? Students should respond now, if not, tell them, "Abdul is painting the gate now." That is why we say painting, because he is doing it now.

4. Ask several students the following questions:
a. What is Zarina doing? Ans. She is cooking.

b. What is the baby doing? Ans. He is crying.

5. Students complete the fill in the blank worksheet with the appropriate words. Do numbers 1 and 2 together as a class. Then have students complete the worksheet individually. Students can refer to the text. See the worksheet on the following page.
6. Choose two students to come up to the white board and write a sentence using a 'now' word as learned in the lesson.

Oral Language: Talk about your favorite sea creature (15 min).

Objective: Students will learn new vocabulary and improve their speaking skills by participating in oral language activities.

1. Arrange students in a pair and tell them to talk about their favorite sea creature. First, demonstrate how they can share by choosing an animal yourself and explaining why it is your favorite. List the following words on the board and say them aloud to help them with their conversation: hermit crab, shark, eel, whale, sea horse, fish, sea lion, seal, and penguin. Students can then follow your example.
2. Make sure to monitor students' conversations and ensure they are speaking in English only.

Writing Block: Complete sea creature descriptions (30 min).

Objective: Students will create their own description.

1. Students complete their descriptions and draw a picture to go with it.
2. Have a few students share their descriptions with the class by reading it aloud.

Grammar Worksheet Present Continuous Tense

Name: ______________ Date: ______________

1. Zarina is ______________the lunch.
2. The baby is ______________.
3. Abdul is ______________the gate.
4. The bird is ______________water from the bowl.
5. The sun is ______________.
6. A man is ______________ the car.
7. Zarina is ______________ to the baby.
8. A girl is ______________ her shopping bag.

Friday

Reading Block: Reading, Spelling, Oral language (60 min).

Reading: Comprehension of *New Oxford* story *Outside and Inside* p.13, A, 2. Fill in the blanks (10 min), Comprehension of Hermit the Crab: Students make a crab tissue art project (25 min).

> *Objective:* Students will be able to write responses to comprehension questions about the story *Outside and Inside* as read in class. Students will understand the story *Hermit the Crab* by completing an art extension activity and by answering comprehension questions orally.

1. Ask students to recall the story we read aloud on Monday, *Outside and Inside*. Ask students to tell you what it was about.
2. Ask students what the different people in the story are doing.
3. Complete fill in the blank activity on p. 13. Do the first two questions with the whole class. Then, let students attempt the last three questions on their own.

   Art Activity: Students will make hermit crabs on chart paper out of tissues as an extension activity to reinforce comprehension of the story. To make the crab art project do the following:

a. Copy the crab template on paper and glue to sturdy chart paper.
b. Have precut small 1 inch squares of red tissue paper ready.
c. Students take a small square of tissue and push it in the center and then twist the bottom. Then, they dip the twisted portion in glue and attach it to the crab.
d. Students repeat step three, covering the whole crab inred tissue paper.
e. Let it dry for a few days. After it is dry you may want to cut the tissue shorter to make the crab look a bit neater.

During the art project, the teacher should consult individually with each student and ask the following questions:

1. Why did Hermit Crab leave his shell?
2. Where did Hermit Crab live?
3. What kind of shells did Hermit Crab find?
4. Why does Hermit Crab like his new shell?
5. How does Hermit Crab realize his new shell is actually his old shell?

6. Is there something that you didn't like that later you realized you really do like?
7. Have you ever been to the sea? What did you see there?

During the above assessment activity, the teacher should make a note which questions each student could easily answer. The teacher will only be able to get to approximately half of the students or less, so in future comprehension check assessments, the teacher should choose different students to check.

Spelling: Spelling Test (15 min).

Objective: Students will learn the spelling of the spelling words by writing them correctly on a spelling test.

1. Students will take a dictation test in which the teacher states each word in a sentence and the students have to write the correct spelling of the given spelling word.
2. Students should only write the spelling word, not the entire sentence.

Teachers may use the following sentences:

1. My **mother** loves me.
2. She took a piece **of** cake.
3. She told the boy to go **out** of the class.
4. The audience will **clap** for the clown.
5. The girl wore a **clip** in her hair.
6. Do not **slam** the door.
7. The boy gave him a **slap** on his face.
8. The boy had only one **chip** left to eat.
9. Did you **drop** your books on the floor?
10. You can hear a **drip** coming from the tap.

Oral Language: *New Oxford* p.13, Questions and answers orally (10 min).

Objective: Students will learn new vocabulary and improve their speaking skills by participating in oral language activities.

1. Ask students to turn to page 12 and 13 of their New Oxford Modern English textbooks.
2. Ask the whole class "*How many plates are there on the table?*" in the picture on page 12. Choose a student to answer. They should say, "*There are 5 plates on the table.*"
3. Explain to students that on page 13 there are 5 different questions in Section 3. Read all the questions, without answers, aloud to the class as they follow along in their books.
4. Tell students that they will work with their partner. One student will read the questions and the other student will answer. They should then switch roles and do it again.
5. The teacher will need to monitor the students and assist some students with reading.

Writing Block: Language Experience Approach: Story about going to the beach (30 min).

Objective: Students will create a story with the help of the teacher and learn how to edit and revise sentences.

1. Take students outside for a walk on the school ground. When outside note different things, such as animals seen, plants observed, and actions taking place.
2. Students should then come inside the class and sit on the carpet in front of the whiteboard. The teacher should explain that we are going to write about what we saw when we went outside today.

3. Ask students what they did and where they went. Choose one student and take his or her sentence. For example, the student may say, "We outside go." The teacher should write the sentence exactly as dictated by the student. Continue with this process until the experience outside is fully described. Make sure to write the sentences exactly as dictated by the students. Do not make any comments on grammar, etc. Only write approximately 4-5 sentences as time is limited.
4. Now go back to the beginning of the story. Look at each sentence and practice revision and editing skills. Look at the first sentence as given in the example. A conversation could proceed as follows:

we go outside

Teacher: Let's look at this sentence *we go outside*. How do you think we could make this sentence better? Who went outside?

Student 1: The students and the teacher.

Teacher: Good, let's add that to our sentence.

the students and the teacher go outside

Teacher: Now where did they go?
Student 2: Outside.
Teacher: Yes, but where outside.
Student 3: We went to the playground.
Teacher: Okay, good, let's add that to our sentence now.

the students and the teacher go outside on the playground

Teacher: Now our sentence is so much better, but something is missing. Do you know what it is?

Student 4: It needs a big T at the beginning and a period at the end.
Teacher: Excellent! Now our sentence is perfect.

The teacher should fix the capital and period and reread the sentence to the class:

The students and the teacher go outside on the playground.

5. Continue with the same process as mentioned in step four with each sentence. Expand sentences with details and correct grammar and punctuation.

6. Have two or three students read the completed story aloud to the class.

Appendix B

EFL Materials List for Pakistan

1. **New Oxford Modern English**
by Nicholas Horsburgh, Oxford University Press, Karachi, 2009: This is a basal series that addresses most strands of English in each unit. It is an adequate and affordable program that teachers can use as a base for their EFL program.

2. **Oxford Reading Tree**
by several different authors, Oxford University Press, Karachi, 2007: This is a reading series that consists of several different individual stories with wonderful pictures and exciting story plots. They are geared towards English language learners and are a great source to use with reading groups or for whole class read-alouds. The series consists of different stages that progress in difficulty. These books are ideal for students from ages 4 to 12 years.

3. **Oxford Literacy Web**
by several different authors, Oxford University Press, Karachi, 2007: This is also a reading series geared towards English language learners and is great for reading groups, individual reading, extensive reading, or class read-alouds. This series consists of several individual stories with lively pictures and interesting plots and can be used with students from ages 4 to 7. This series also consists of different stages that progress in difficulty.

4. **Oxford Progressive English Readers**
by several different authors, Oxford University Press, Karachi, 2007: This is a series of English readers for students ages 8 to 14 and consists of six different levels. There are many classics included in this series that have been adapted to the needs of English learners. Some titles include: *Little Women,*

The Wizard of Oz, and Treasure Island. These stories are great to use as part of small reading groups, individual reading, or an extensive reading program.

5. **The Magic Factory Series**
by Theresa Breslin, Oxford University Press, Karachi, 2007: This is a fictional series of stories about a messy witch that works at a magic factory. This series is a lot of fun and full of captivating illustrations. Beginning readers are sure to become enchanted and fall in love with reading. This series is good to use in classes II to VI as part of reading groups, individual reading, an extensive reading program,or as a whole class read-aloud.

6. **Oxford Very First Dictionary**
Oxford University Press, Karachi, 2007: This is a colorful dictionary easy to use for students ages 4 and up. This dictionary has over 300 words and introduces students to the basic concepts of how to use a dictionary.

7. **Journeys**
Oxford University Press, Karachi, 2007: This is a non-fiction series about plants, animals and the universe. It is full of vibrant photographs and engaging text. This series is appropriate for students ages 8 and up. It can be used as part of reading groups, individual reading, an extensive reading program, or as a whole class read-aloud.

Appendix C

Useful EFL Websites

1. http://a4esl.org/
   This website has grammar and vocabulary quizzes that can be used with students in classes IV to VI. There are also bilingual quizzes with Urdu and English. Also, teachers can create new bilingual quizzes for use by others on the internet.

2. http://pbskids.org/
   This site has several different activities that are based on popular children's cartoons. Students can read stories, play games, listen music, and watch videos.

3. http://www.english-4kids.com/
   This is an English learning site for young learners that offers printable worksheets, video lessons, powerpoint lessons, coloring worksheets and games.

4. http://www.tlsbooks.com/englishworksheets.htm
   This site offers printable worksheets for English learning on several different English topics for students in classes I to V.

5. http://www.eslkidslab.com/
   This site offers video lessons by course, printable worksheets, self grading exercises, flashcards, phonics materials, and teaching tips.

6. http://www.mes-english.com/phonics.php
   This site offers flashcards, game cards, board games, handouts, and worksheets all based on phonics concepts.

7. http://www.esl4kids.net/
   This is a great site for young learners and offers games, songs,

fingerplays, action rhymes, craft ideas, printable materials, tongue twisters and phonics materials.

8. http://www.britishcouncil.org/kids
   This site is for learners of all ages and offers stories to read and listen, games, songs, and flash cards.

9. http://www.netrover.com/~kingskid/108.html
   This is a great site that offers stories to read and listen including stories that use sight words, phonemic awareness games, sight word drill games, vowel games, learn to type games, writing activities, word search games, interactive writing, Dolch sight word games, spelling games, editing games, grammar games, and rhyming games to name a few.

10. http://www.superteacherworksheets.com/phonics.html
    This site offers teachers several different readymade worksheets on phonics. A range of phonic concepts are covered from blends to vowel dipthongs and digraphs.

GLOSSARY

active listening A skill students use when learning in which they demonstrate attentive listening by performing some action such as the raise of a thumb or a *yes* or *no* answer to a question, etc.

antonyms Pair of words which have opposite meanings.

authentic literature Literature that provides an interesting and engaging story.

author's chair When a student acts like the author and reads aloud his own composition in front of the class.

automaticity The act of recognizing and understanding words quickly and efficiently so that very little effort is needed to do so.

background knowledge The knowledge a student has about any given subject before instruction begins that helps aid the student in understanding new material.

balanced approach A strategy to teach reading that is based on teaching reading with phonics as well as the whole language approach where students memorize lines of text and are exposed to authentic literature.

basal program A reading program that includes instruction in all areas of English instruction including reading, grammar, vocabulary, spelling, and writing. Most basal programs do not include high quality literature.

beginning, middle and end maps A map that shows three boxes, one for the beginning, one for the middle and one for the end of a story. Students retell a story by drawing pictures and writing text for each of the three different parts of a story.

blending When sounds of a word are put together in order to create the sound of the whole word.

blends A phonic term that refers to two letters that are together in a word in which the sound of both the letters can be heard and they are said together, i.e., *bl* as in black, *cl* as in clock, *st* as in stamp.

comprehensible input A term developed by Krashen which refers to teaching practices that specifically help English language learners acquire English more easily, i.e., use visuals, speak slowly, etc.

context The text which someone reads and typically refers to; the meaning behind what someone reads.

context skills The ability to understand a word, based on the meaning of the surrounding text.

continuous writing Writing in paragraph form rather than in points, bullets or outline form.

cooperative learning Learning in which students work in small groups with other students in order to learn a given concept.

dialogue journals The students use to communicate with the teacher about class work, social interactions, or interesting literature read in class, etc.

digraphs A phonic term that represents two letters together in a word which makes up one sound which is different from the individual letters, i.e., *sh, wh, ch,* etc.

explicit learning Learning in which a specific concept is the objective of a lesson and students are directly taught the given concept.

expository text Informational text which often times is seen in content area classes such as science and social studies.

felt board A board made from a soft cloth material that is posted on a hard board. Story characters are then cut from the same cloth and are posted on the board in order to retell a story to students. Students often retell stories themselves using the characters on the board.

fluency Refers to the ease and quickness in which a student reads a text with proper intonation and phrasing.

gist Refers to when someone tries to understand the overall meaning of something they read. Also a comprehension strategy in which a small group of students create a summary statement about a small portion of text they have read.

high frequency words Words encountered most frequently when one reads a text. High frequency words typically do not follow phonics patterns and need to be memorized, i.e., *know.*

homographs A pair of words that are spelled alike but have different sounds and meanings.

homonym A pair of words that sound alike and are spelled alike, but have different meanings.

homophones A pair of words that sound alike, but have different spellings and meanings.

idiom An expression that means something different than the words that make up the expression and are commonly known by people whose native language is the same as the given idiom.

IELTS An examination recognized worldwide that tests English language learners on English language skills.

implicit learning Learning in which students learn slowly through a natural process of acquisition. A specific objective is not taught. Extensive reading is one way to improve implicit learning of vocabulary.

intonation The manner in which one's voice rises and falls as he or she reads text.

KWL chart A chart that is usually used with expository text and demonstrates what students know, want to know and what they have learned.

Language experience approach An approach to teaching writing in which the teacher guides a group of students in creating a story based on an actual experience students have had.

lexical Vocabulary

literature circles Small groups that meet to discuss and complete activities associated with a specific piece of literature.

mini lesson A small lesson on a specific objective. Often times, it lasts approximately five minutes or less.

native language The language one first learns to understand and converse in.

onsets The beginning letter/s of a word before the first vowel.

pantomime The actions done by hand and body gestures to represent some meaning.

paraphrasing Rewording text or spoken language.

participatory learning Learning in which students offer some feedback to the teacher throughout the lesson.

pen pals A pair of people who correspond in written form either through post or email. Often used in EFL classes to help students improve their language skills.

personal dictionaries A dictionary created by a student in which a student includes new words as he or she learns them.

phonemic awareness The ability to understand that words are made up of sounds and those sounds can be manipulated.

phonics The study of words and letters and their associated sounds.

phrases of negotiation Simple phrases that are used in conversations to help those involved understand what the conversation is about.

phrasing The manner in which one says different sentences.
plot The events of a story.

positive reinforcement The use of positive words to help reinforce good or proficient behavior.

problem The conflict in a story.

Readers Theater A play which is read from a script where very little props are used. Students often practice reading repeatedly in order to prepare for a performance.

rimes The end of rhyming words. The vowel and following consonants in the last syllable of a word.

role play A small play created by students either done with a script created by students or improvised as the role play proceeds.

scan When a student quickly goes over material in search for specific information.

segmenting Dividing words into their different syllables in order to help read or understand the word.

setting A literary term that refers to the time and place in which a story takes place.

sight words Words in a text that students should automatically recognize during reading, rather than try and decode them.

skim When a student quickly goes through the text to obtain an overall meaning of what the text will be about.

slang Words or expressions in language that are used to represent some meaning other than the literal meaning of the words used.

spelling collages A collage in which spelling words are cut from magazines or pictures and posted on a chart. The entire chart is covered in clippings of different spelling words so that none of the chart can be seen.

story maps A map that can be used to help understand the organization of a story and includes characters, setting, plot/events, and conclusion/resolution.

structural analysis When one breaks a word up and looks at its different parts, such as a prefix, suffix, root, or syllables.

syllable A unit of spoken language. The word *football* has two syllables.

synonyms A pair of words that have similar meanings.

syntactic skills A strategy used when one tries to understand words during reading that involves the use of substituting an appropriate word that would fit grammatically in a sentence.

syntax The grammatical arrangement of words in a sentence.

synthesizing When one connects parts of a word together in order to figure out what a word is.

task-based learning Oral language learning in which students complete different types of tasks in order to improve their oral language skills.

temporary spelling The spelling students use as they first begin to learn how to spell and often shows beginning stages of understanding phonics.

text genres The different types of text that are available. For example, science fiction, fiction, expository, fantasy, riddle books, newspapers, menus, etc.

TOEFL An examination recognized worldwide that tests English language learners' English skills.

total physical response Developed by Asher (1982), an approach to EFL education in which a teacher helps a student to learn English through the use of physical movement with words.

venn diagram A two circle diagram in which the two circles connect and form a third space. The diagram shows how two separate topics are different in the far two spaces and how they are the same in the middle space.

visuals A term used in EFL education that refers to charts, pictures, and/or actual objects used to represent different words or expressions.

vowel clusters The combination of two or more different vowels together that form a unique sound, often times much different than the individual letters.

word wall A wall of words in a classroom which contains words that students should understand the meanings of, as well as know the spellings of. Word walls can be on specific topics of interest such as the sea or word walls can consist of high frequency or sight words students need to learn.

writing process The steps one proceeds through when he or she writes a composition: prewriting, drafting, revising, editing, publishing.

writing workshop A writing workshop is where students are given time in a classroom to write their own compositions and proceed through the writing process with the help of the teacher. Often the writing workshop includes mini lessons on a range of writing topics to help students improve their writing.

REFERENCES

Asato, M. (2003). *Challenge and change for EFL oral communication instruction.* R esearch project. Koyo Senior High School, Okinawa, Japan in conjunction with Georgetown University. Retrieved January 15, 2009 from ERIC database.

Bamford, J. & Day, R. (1997). Extensive reading: What is it? Why bother? *The Language Teacher. 21*(5), 1-6. Retrieved February 7, 2009, from http://jaltpublications.org/tlt/files/97/may/extensive. html

Bear, D., Invenizzi, M., Templeton, S., & Johnston, F. (1996).

Words their way. Word study for phonics, vocabulary, and spelling. Upper Saddle River, NJ: Prentice Hall.

Beglar, D., & Hunt, A. (2005). A framework for developing EFL reading vocabulary. *Reading in a foreign language, 17*(1), 23-59.

Boucher, E., & Leong, P. (2002). Theater in the classroom: Using readers theater to improve EFL learners' oral skills. *The English Teacher, An International Journal, 5*(3), 230-24

British Council. (2004). *Worldwide survey of primary ELT- teaching English to young learners.* Retrieved February 6, 2009, from http://www.britishcouncil.org /english/eyl/index.html

Gersten, R. et al. (2007).*Effective literacy and English language instruction for English learners in the elementary grades. IES Practice Guide (NCEE2007-4011).* Washington, DC: National Center for Education Evaluation and Regional Assistance, Institute of Education Sciences, U.S. Dept of Education. Retrieved February 5, 2009, from http://ies.ed.gov/ncee

Ghare, M. (2007). Creative writing prompts. *Buzzle.com website.* Retrieved May 10, 2009, from http://www.buzzle.com/articles/creative-writing-prompts.html

Gipe, J. (2006). *Multiple paths to literacy. Assessment and differentiated instruction for diverse learners, K-12* (6th ed.). Upper Saddle River, NJ: Pearson Education.

Gray, R. (2004).Grammar correction in the ESL/EFL writing classes may not be effective. *The Internet TESL Journal, 10*(11), 1-5. Retrieved February 5, 2009, from http://itselj.org/techniques/ gray-writingcorrection.html

Harvey, S., & Goudvis, A. (2007). *Strategies that work. Teaching compr-ehension for understanding and engagement* (2nd ed.). Portland, OR: Stenhouse.

Horsburgh, N. (2009). *New Oxford modern English.* Karachi, Pakistan: Oxford University Press.

Huber, J. (2004). A closer look at SQ3R. *Reading Improvement, 41*(2), 108-112.

Kotapish, C. (1993). *The place of grammar in the ESL/EFL classroom* An annotated bibliography. Indiana University of Pennsylvania. Retrieved January 15, 2009, from ERIC database.

Lundblade, S. (1994). *Invented spelling in the writing process: Applications for the elementary EFL/ESL classroom.* Masters Thesis. Biola University. Retrieved January 15, 2009, from ERIC database.

Mitton, T. (1999). *Cheeky fish.* Hong Kong: Oxford University Press.